Savory's Southern Specialties

Fifty Family Favorites

By, Sheri Savory and Dakota Workman

Love "canning your own food? Sheri recommends, Rebel Canners Cookbook, by Tammy McNeill

NOTES:

Contents

Dedication

Patti McNeil (on the left) was the author of the recipe cards and Her daughter Sheri (on the right) to preserve these Southern Specialties.

I dedicate this exclusive collection of my family recipes to future generations in my family and my granddaughters Chef Dakota and Chef Demetra who are my motivation and my heart! My mother sat down, and hand wrote this collection for me, and I am sharing it with the world because the traditions and generations behind these creations are among the earliest Colonial and Pioneer families in America. My mom's family is part of the fabric of the "American South," and we are proud of our heritage. We are ecstatic to have this opportunity to bring these recipes into your family's kitchen.

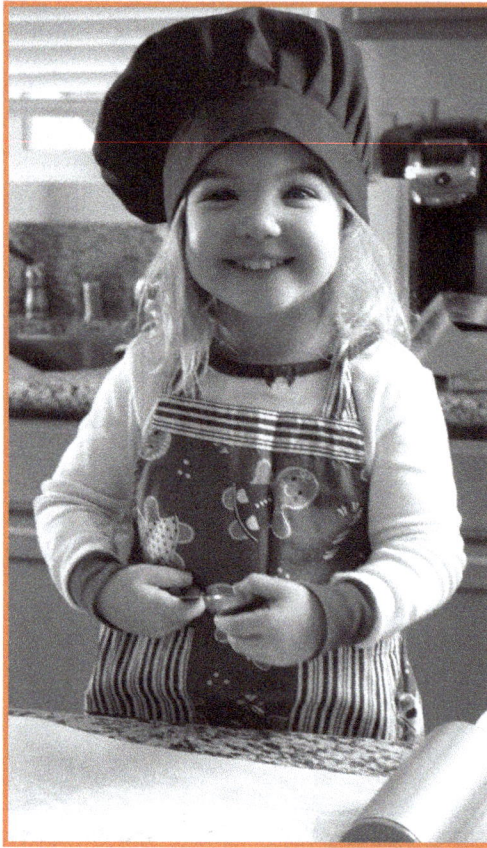

My family has a long tradition in Southern baking. We descend from English, Irish, Scottish, Scandinavian and Native Americans. We were early pioneers in the "American South," and many were American Colonists. Tracing my family genealogy for over thirty years gives me personal insight into the women behind these recipes. My mother preserved them to her best knowledge, and I have included her handwritten recipe cards. She had such beautiful handwriting, and her emotion comes through in the directions she relays.

We all have unique meals that we prepare as we gather to dine on specific foods to celebrate family traditions or start new ones. In my family, we have different memories that each can share about particular items. My cousin and I shared the love of a chocolate cake that we called "Grandma Cake," but each of us preferred a different frosting. My grandma would make sure to cater to our favorite variation for our birthday parties. Developing a baking style and signature is motivation to share future stories with your loved ones.

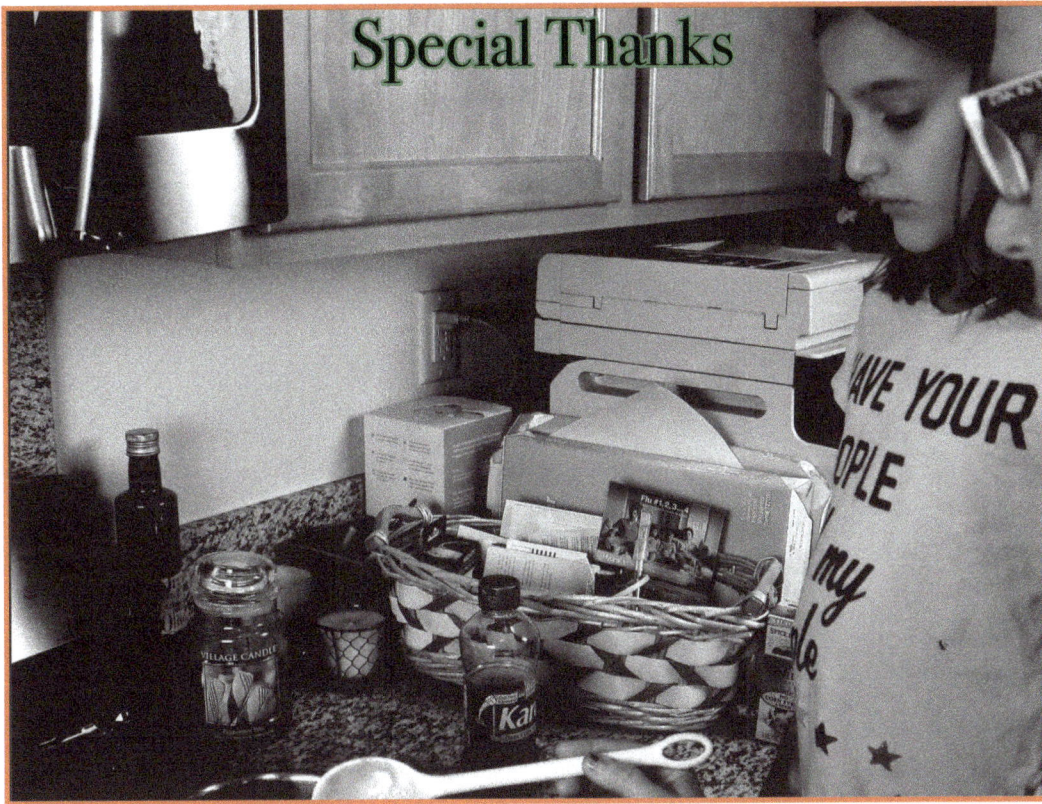
Special Thanks

Dakota and I have discovered that our cookbook is a great fundraiser for nonprofit organizations or special events!

My granddaughter Dakota indeed has a gift for cooking, baking and decorating. She and her Grandma have cooked together consistently since she was one year old. She has taught her little sister many techniques and will undoubtedly be the person everyone in the family will call for cooking advise. She created 40% of these recipes and is proud to have been such a big part of this cookbook. Dakota's little sister, Demetra did her best to roll out the dough, clean up messes, make messes and smile pretty for photos. Her contribution was much appreciated. Many thanks to Rochelle Savory for the use of her kitchen and her patience were long-suffering as it took many months to plan, scan, shop, stock supplies, prepare, store and photograph all of the recipes. She has always stood by my side, and this book is my gift to her as she is the keeper of our memories, books, and keepsakes. I wanted her to have a modern, easy way to access all of her beloved recipes without depending on physical cards that could someday get destroyed and lost forever.

Send a copy/photo of your book receipt to savoryssouthernspecialties@gmail.com and receive a set our recipe cards.

2 doz medium apples, quartered
2 qts. sweet cider
3 c sugar
1 1/2 tsp ground cinnamon
1/2 tsp ground cloves

Cook apples in cider until tender.
Press through a sieve or food mill (or
simply mash) Cook pulp until
thick enough to mound ~~up~~ in a
spoon. As pulp thickens
stir frequently to prevent sticking.
Add sugar & spice. Cook slowly,
until thick, stirring frequently.
About 1 hr. (Can put in oven in
heavy roaster.)
Pour hot into hot jars leaving
1/4" head space. Adjust tops
seals hot.

Condiments

01. Apple Butter-Old Fashioned

Good Old-Fashioned Apple Butter just like grandma made. Apple butter has been a staple in many homes with roots in the "American South" for generations. A favorite of young and old alike.

Intermediate   90-Minutes

Ingredients

2 dozen medium apples, quartered
2 quarts sweet cider
3 cups sugar
1/2 teaspoon ground cinnamon
1/2 teaspoon ground cloves

Preparation

Cook apples in cider until tender. Press through a sieve or food mill/processor (or simply mash.) Cook pulp until thick enough to round up into a spoon. As pulp thickens stir frequently to prevent sticking. Add sugar and spice. Cook slowly until thick, stirring frequently. About 1 hour (can put in the oven in heavy roaster.) Pour hot, into hot jars leaving 1/4-inch head space. Adjust top seals hot!

My Two Cents

The mix of cinnamon and cloves makes a delicious treat on hot homemade bread, biscuits or toast. Use your imagination as you will love the simple yet robust flavor of this traditional delight. Grandmas in our family would can this and give it out as gifts for the holidays. We all loved seeing the Mason jar was in our stockings at Christmas. What a scrumptious blend of sweet apples, cider, and spices that make this easy recipe explode on your taste buds.

1 32 oz bottle Ketsup
1/2 c Worcheshire Sauce
1/2 c Vinegar
2-3 drops hat sauce (Tabasco)
1 c Brown Sugar
1 tsp Red Pepper
1 tsp Black Pepper
Add 2 c water
Simmer till thick —   over
  Optional   1 oz liquid Smoke

02. Bar B Cue Sauce-Robust-Easy

"Pop" was my mom's stepfather, and he made these thick hamburgers with his homemade bar b cue sauce, and it is out of this world.

 Intermediate  90-Minutes

Ingredients

1 32 oz. bottle ketchup

1/2 cup Worcheshire sauce

2-3 drops hot sauce (Tabasco)

1 cup brown sugar

1 teaspoon red pepper

1 teaspoon black pepper

2 cups water

1 oz liquid smoke (optional)

Preparation

Simmer till thick!

My Two Cents

Robust is the word that came to mind as I taste tested this authentic creation. It will become your favorite item to add to your cookout menu. I am confident once you introduce it to your friends and family you won't want to buy pre-made sauce ever again. This sauce is so tasty I can't say enough about it!

NOTES:

_____

_____

_____

_____

_____

12 or 14 medium cucumbers

3/4 c salt   3 T celery seed
6 1/2 qts water   1/4 c white mustard seed
7 c Sugar   1 tsp. Turmeric
6 c White Vinegar

Wash cucumbers & slice. Soak
over night in brine made by disolving the
6 qts water & 3/4 c salt reserving 1/2 qt water
for vinegar. Drain brine off & discard.
Mix sugar, vinegar & the 1/2 qt water &
spices in large pan, bring to a
boil & boil 3 minutes. Add cucumbers
& boil 10 minutes. Fill hot,
sterilized jars. Seal at once!

Green pepper, sliced onions &
cauliflower may be used with
cucumbers if desired.

12

03. Bread and Butter Pickles-Classic

My grandmother's recipe is a "sweet pickle" that I know to be described as a taste in between a sweet and dill pickle. The family will wait in anticipation of the season when cucumbers are in season allowing the canning of this one of a kind pickle to commence.

Intermediate   120-Minutes

Ingredients

12 or 14 medium cucumbers

3/4 cups salt

3 tablespoons celery seed

5 1/2 quarts water

1/4 cups white mustard seed

7 cups sugar

1 teaspoon turmeric

5 cups white vinegar

Preparation

Cook apples in cider until tender. Press through a sieve or food mill/processor (or simply mash.) Cook pulp until thick enough to round up into a spoon. As pulp thickens stir frequently to prevent sticking. Add sugar and spice. Cook slowly until thick, stirring frequently. About 1 hour (can put in the oven in heavy roaster.) Pour hot, into hot jars leaving 1/4-inch head space. Adjust top seals hot!

My Two Cents

The mix of cinnamon and cloves makes a delicious treat on hot homemade bread, biscuits or toast. Use your imagination as you will love the simple yet robust flavor of this traditional delight. Grandmas in our family would can this and give it out as gifts for the holidays. We all loved seeing the Mason jar was in our stockings at Christmas. What a scrumptious blend of sweet apples, cider, and spices that make this easy recipe explode on your taste buds.

Preheat Oven 400°

Mix together: 1/2 c soft shortening or butter
1 c sugar
1 egg

1 T grated orange rind (optional) Stir
in 2 1/2 c flour, 1 tsp soda 1/2 tsp salt.
Stir in, 1 1/2 tsp. cinnamon 1 1/2 tsp
nutmeg, Mix with both hands,
1 c. seedless raisins, 1 c. mixed
candied fruits & 1/2 c chopped nuts.

Divide dough in half. Chill.
Roll one half at a time on board
into a rectangle. Cut in 2" strips.
Bake on lightly greased cookie
sheet 10-12 min. While warm
spread with confectioners sugar
icing. Cut baked strips into bars.
Very good!

04. Frosted Fruit Bars-Very Good

Bars are one of my favorites to make. Rich in antioxidants with all the fruit, it lends to the moistness of this item.

 Easy

 45-Minutes

Ingredients

Mix together

1/2 cup soft shortening or butter

1 cup sugar

1 egg

1 tablespoon grated orange rind (optional)

Stir in:

2 1/2 cups flour

1 teaspoon soda

1/2 teaspoon salt

Stir in:

1/2 teaspoon cinnamon

1/2 teaspoon nutmeg

Mix with both hands:

1 cup seedless raisins

1 cup mixed candied fruits

1/2 cup chopped nuts

Preparation

Preheat oven to 400 degrees. Mix together butter, sugar, egg and orange rind (optional.) Stir in flour, soda and salt then stir in cinnamon and nutmeg. Mix with both hands raisins, candied fruits, and nuts. Divide dough in half. Chill. Roll one half at a time on board into a rectangle. Cut in 2" strips. Bake on lightly greased cookie sheet 10-12 min. While warm spread with confectioners' sugar icing. Cut baked strips into bars. Good!

My Two Cents

This bar is a perfect treat for the health-conscious individuals in your life. A cup of tea or coffee is the ideal complement to this recipe. These are chocked full of nutritional ingredients with a great texture. You will love the way the frosting brings out the flavor in this bar.

NOTES:

_____

Frosted Fruit Bars

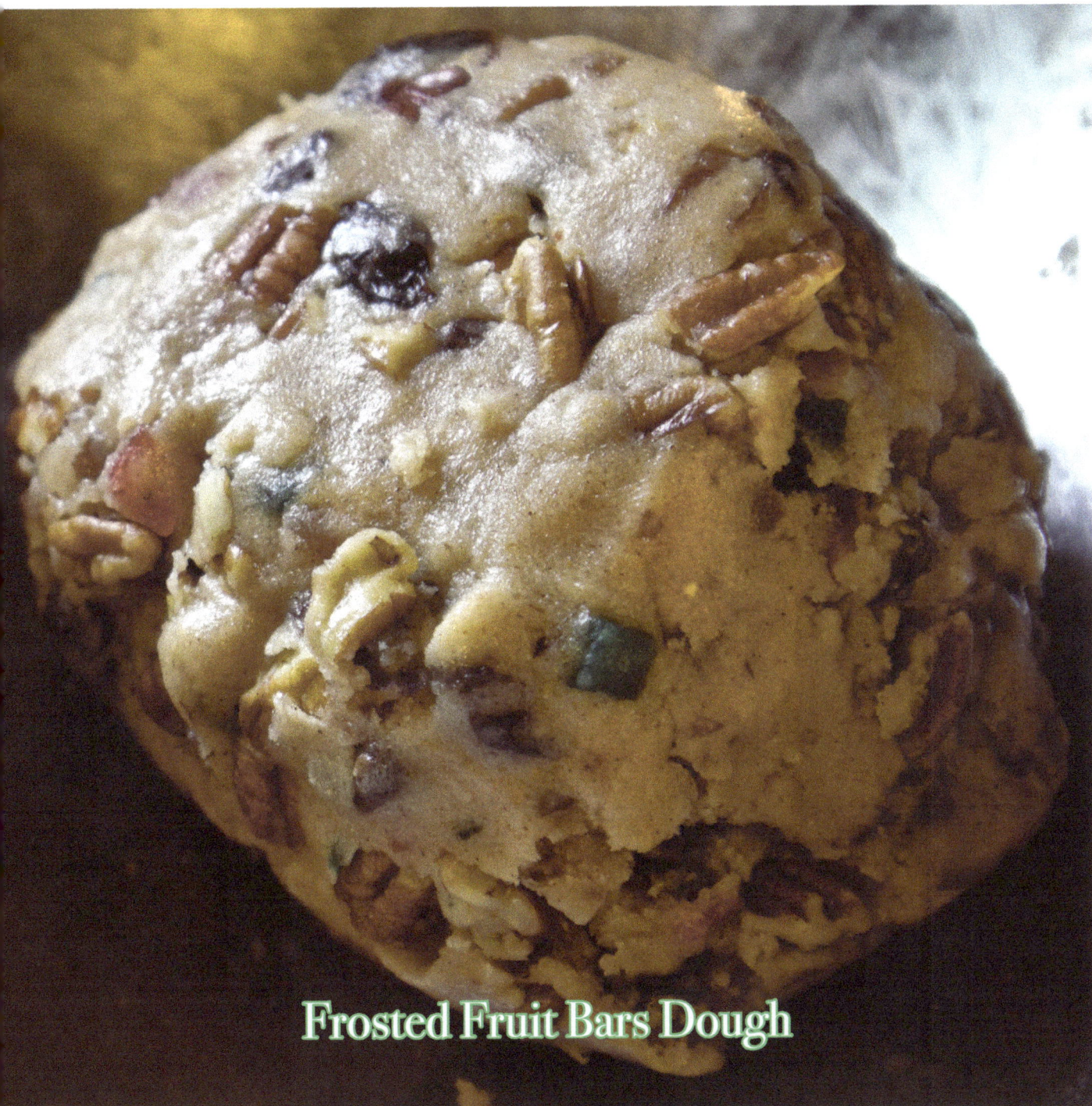

Frosted Fruit Bars Dough

4 eggs separated
2 1/4 c packed brown sugar
1 T water
1 tsp vanilla
2 c sifted flour
1 tsp baking powder
1/2 tsp salt
1 c gumdrops, cut fine
3/4 c chopped walnuts

1. Beat egg yolks, then add sugar, water & vanilla. Mix well.
2. Sift flour with baking powder & salt. Stir into first mixture. Then stir in gumdrops & nuts
3. Beat egg whites until stiff but not dry. Stir into batter. Spread in well greased oblong pan 13×9×2".
4. Bake in preheated 350° oven 30-35 min. Cut into bars while still warm.
   Makes 3 dozen

05. Gumdrop Cookies-Colorful

You will enjoy passing this along to future generations. Share the joy of creating this with your loved ones and start a new tradition.

 Intermediate

 120-Minutes

Ingredients

4 eggs (separated)

2 1/4 cup brown sugar (packed)

1 tablespoon water

1 teaspoon vanilla

2 cups sifted flour

1 teaspoon baking powder

1/2 teaspoon salt

1 cup gumdrop, cut fine

3/4 cups chopped walnuts

Preparation

Beat egg yolks, then add sugar, water, and vanilla. Mix well. Sift flour with baking powder and salt. Stir into the first mixture. Then stir in gumdrops and nuts. Beat egg whites until stiff but not dry, Stir into batter. Spread in well-greased oblong pan 13x9x2. Bake in preheated 350 degree oven 30-35 minutes. Cut into bars while still warm. Makes 3 dozen bars.

My Two Cents

The colors in these gumdrop cookies make the bars a fantastic addition to your holiday platters, tins or in a cookie exchange.

NOTES:

_____

_____

_____

1 pkg. mince meat
1 can Eagle Brand Milk
1 c graham cracker crumbs. (about
15 crackers ground very finely)
Blend all ingredients + pour into a
greased 8" square pan.
Bake 360° for 30 minutes. Cut
into squares when cool.

06. New England Bars-Mincemeat

This bar takes me back in time and reminds me of flavors of yesteryear. A taste no doubt brought to American from the Old World.

 Easy

 45-Minutes

Ingredients

- package mincemeat
- can sweetened condensed milk
- cup graham cracker crumbs (about 15 crackers ground very finely.)

Preparation

Blend all ingredients and pour into a greased 8" square pan. Bake at 350 degrees for 30 minutes. Cut into squares when cool.

My Two Cents

I love the taste of minced meat! It adds an unmistakable flavor and texture to a classic holiday cookie. The spice and aroma are divine. This recipe takes me back to grandma's house.

NOTES:

_____
_____
_____
_____
_____
_____

1 c soft real butter
1/2 c sifted confectioners sugar
1 tsp vanilla
2 1/4 c sifted flour
1/4 tsp salt
3/4 c finely chopped nuts

chill dough 1 hour. Roll into balls. Bake on ungreased cookie sheet 400° 10-12 minutes. Roll in powdered sugar.

Makes 4 doz cookies

07. Holiday Nut Balls-Favorite

These melt in your mouth with the crunch of the nuts and sweetness of the powder sugar these are always a hit.

 Easy

 45-Minutes

Ingredients

1 cup soft REAL butter

1/2 cup sifted confectioners sugar

1 teaspoon vanilla

2 1/4 cups sifted flour

1/4 teaspoon salt

3/4 cup finely chopped nuts

Preparation

Chill dough 1 hour. Roll into balls. Bake at 400 degrees on an ungreased cookie sheet for 10-12 minutes. Roll in powdered sugar. Makes 4 dozen balls.

My Two Cents

Covered with confectioners' sugar these mouth-watering cookies melt as they touch your taste buds. A light biscuit is a grand addition to your baked goods anytime. It is a traditional find during the holiday season. A must-have in your tins, platters and at any cookie exchange.

NOTES:

_____

_____

_____

_____

_____

Banana Bread

1 c. sugar
1/2 c. margarine
2 eggs
3 T water
4 small ripe bananas
2 c flour
1 tsp soda
1 c Pecans (optional)
Bake in loaf pans. 350° 45 minutes
Makes 2 loaves

Breads

o8. Banana Bread–Moist

Everyone loves banana bread so be sure to make a few extra loaves to ensure you have enough to give away and a couple to keep for yourself.

 Easy

 45-Minutes

Ingredients

1 cup sugar

1/2 cup butter or margarine

2 eggs

3 tablespoons water

4 small ripe bananas

2 cups flour

1 teaspoon soda

1 cup pecans (optional)

Preparation

Cream, butter, sugar, and eggs first. Peel Bananas or Zucchinis. Mix remaining Ingredients adding pecans last. Bake in loaf pans at 350 degrees for 45 minutes. Makes 2 small loaves.

My Two Cents

There is nothing like a warm fire when the brisk wind blows outside in the autumn. Old-Fashioned Banana Bread can be added to a goodie tray for a holiday meal or sliced individually and put into the freezer to have a handy breakfast or mid-day snack. In a family of bakers, many variations of this have been made. Walnuts are a traditional addition, but raisins, cranberries or pecans may be your style. This is a thoughtful gift that packaged nicely will wow the most discriminating of audiences.

NOTES:

----

1 1/2 c yellow corn meal	2 eggs
1 T. Flour (heaping)	1 small can Creamed Corn
3 tsp. salt	3 Jalapeno Peppers
1/2 tsp soda	1/2 green pepper (chopped)
1 C buttermilk	4-5 Green Onions chopped
1/2 c. oil	1 1/2 c. grated cheese cheddar

Mix corn meal, flour, salt + soda. Add buttermilk, oil, eggs + corn. Stir in Chopped Jalapeno, green pepper, onion. Pour into pan 1/2 of batter (Pan has been heated with 2 tsp. oil). Sprinkle with cheese. Repeat process.

Bake 375 for 30 min.

28

09. Mexican Cornbread-Wonderful

What a complex combination of flavor. The texture divine and this dish is like a meal in itself. Enjoy serving this delightful cornbread to your friends and family.

Intermediate   45-Minutes

Ingredients

1/2 cups yellow cornmeal

1 tablespoon flour (heaping)

3 teaspoons salt

1/2 teaspoon soda

1 cup buttermilk

1/2 cup oil

2 eggs

1 small can cream corn

3 jalapeño peppers

1/2 green pepper (chopped)

4-5 green onions chopped

1 1/2 cup grated cheddar cheese

Preparation

Mix cornmeal, flour, salt, and soda. Add buttermilk, oil, eggs, and corn. Stir in chopped jalapeño, green pepper, onion. Pour into pan 1/2 of the batter (pan has to be heated with two teaspoons oil.) Sprinkle with cheese. Repeat process. Bake 375 degrees for 30 minutes.

My Two Cents

The flavors combine in this cornbread bringing out all the taste of the peppers. Cheese and buttermilk ensure the texture will be creamy and perfect.

NOTES:

----

3 c. Sugar   1½

3 c. Flour

1½ tsp salt

½ tsp cloves   }   Sift together

1 tsp cinnamon

½ t nutmeg

   4 egg beaten

1 large can of pumpkin (17 oz)

½ c oil   2 tsp. soda (mix in 3 T water)

1 c nuts   1 c raisins   Beat.

Makes 2 loaves.   350°

Grease + flour pans.

Applesauce can be used
instead of pumpkin.

10. Pumpkin Bread-Festive

The house will smell of spices and pumpkin that will draw a crowd when you make this bread.

 Easy

 90-Minutes

Ingredients

3 cups sugar

3 cups flour

1 1/2 teaspoons salt

1/2 teaspoon cloves

1 teaspoon cinnamon

1/2 teaspoons nutmeg

4 eggs beaten

1 large can of pumpkin (17 oz pumpkin meat)

1/2 cup oil

2 teaspoons soda (mix in 3 tablespoons water)

1 cup raisins

1 cup nuts

Preparation

Combine all ingredients in a bowl beating until mixed. Makes 2 loaves. Grease and flour pans. Applesauce can be used instead of pumpkin.

My Two Cents

Everyone loves this bread with the spices and soft nature of it. Served hot with butter, toasted in the morning or sliced cold anytime. Add raisins, nuts or dates to satisfy your style. Your friends and family will praise your baking skills with their first bite.

NOTES:

Pumpkin Bread

1 1/2 C Sugar
1/2 C Crisco
2 C applesauce
2 eggs
2 1/2 C flour
1 tsp salt
2 tsp soda   1/2 C raisins
1 tsp Cinnamon   1/2 tsp Cloves 1 C nuts

Bake 325° 1 hr –

34

Cakes and Cobblers

11. Applesauce Cake-Incredible

What a scrumptious and moist cake this is. Step back in time with the wholesome taste and unique flavor of this treat.

 Easy

 90-Minutes

Ingredients

1 1/2 cups sugar

1/2 cup shortening

2 cups applesauce

2 eggs

2 1/2 cups flour

1 teaspoon salt

2 teaspoons soda

1/2 cup raisins

1 teaspoon cinnamon

1/2 teaspoon cloves

1 cup nuts

Preparation

Bake 325 degrees for one hour.

My Two Cents

My great grandmothers were born in the late 1800s in Indian Territory. Keep in mind that the industrial revolution began in the 1900s, so the pace of life in the American South and Midwest was slow. It took half the day to walk to work across the mountain for some. Sweets found their way into the kitchen through natural ingredients like fruit, and the ever so moist texture of applesauce was hard to beat. Sitting down to dessert after a long day in the field would be the opportunity a woman waited for to warm the hearts of her loved ones. A slice of this cake was heaven on the dry plains of Oklahoma. The red dirt blew fiercely during the dust bowl and cooking was a challenge. Keep this in mind, it was at the end of the land distribution in Oklahoma, and they struggled to divide the land. Indians and Cowboys haggled over a "Cup of Joe" and a slice of cake with some sweet cream to negotiate their legacy.

3 c. flour
2 c sugar
1 tsp soda
1 tsp salt } Sift together

1 tsp Cinnamon

Add   1 c. oil
       2 c. ground, grated carrots
       1 c. nuts
       1 sm. can crushed pineapple

Beat 2 minutes on medium
speed.
Pour into greased cake pan,
(Looks pretty when cooked in
Angle Food pan.   Cook 350°°
    45° — 1 hour.
Frost with a Philly cream
cheese frosting.

12. Carrot Cake-Heavenly

Nothing better than a slice of heaven like this decadent carrot cake. It is a moist cake chalked full of spices, nuts, and carrots. You will love this prize-winning recipe and will be proud to serve it to your guests.

Intermediate   90-Minutes

Ingredients

- cups flour
- cups sugar
- teaspoon soda
- teaspoon salt
- teaspoon cinnamon
- cup oil
- cups ground, grated carrots
- cup nuts
- small can crushed pineapple

Preparation

Sift together flour, sugar, soda, salt, cinnamon. Add oil, carrots, nuts, and pineapple. Beat for two minutes on medium speed. Pour into a greased cake pan (looks pretty when cooked in an Angel food pan.) Bake at 350 degrees for 45 minutes-1 hour. Frost with cream cheese frosting.

My Two Cents

There is nothing better than a homemade carrot cake, in my opinion. Frosted with your favorite cream cheese frosting to add that tangy contrast to the not-too-sweet taste of the carrots. The pineapple insures its moisture and nuts lends an organic flare to your masterpiece. Win the prize for the family favorite each time you make this. My great grandmother brought this to church functions, birthdays, reunions and holiday dinners and it is a sure win any time of the year.

2 c flour } Bring to a boil.
2 c sugar }
   Add 2 cubes oleo or margarine
   1 C water & 3 1/2 T cocoa.
Cool slightly.
   Add 2 eggs 1/2 c buttermilk.
   1 tsp soda, 1 tsp vanilla
Bake in sheet pan. 400° 20 minutes

13. Chocolate Cake-Tantalizing

This recipe is for what my family knows as "Grandma Cake" which in my opinion is the best cake you can ever make. My grandma made this for me on my birthday, and I looked forward to going to her house for this fudgy sweet.

Intermediate   45-Minutes

Ingredients

2 cups flour

2 cups sugar

1/2 cups, 2 sticks of butter (margarine)

1 cup water

3 1/2 tablespoons cocoa

2 eggs

1/2 cup buttermilk

1 teaspoon soda

1 teaspoon vanilla

Preparation

In a saucepan bring to a boil flour, sugar, butter, water, and cocoa. Cool slightly. Add 2 eggs, buttermilk, soda and vanilla. Bake in a sheet pan at 400 degrees for 20 minutes.

Icing

1 cube oleo
3 T Cocoa
6 T milk

Bring to boil. Remove from fire. Add 1 Box powdered sugar, 1 c nuts & 1 tsp vanilla. mix. Spread over hot cake as soon as its out of the oven.

13 b. Chocolate Cake Icing-Creamy

This icing is fudgy and delicious.

 Easy

 30-Minutes

Ingredients

1/4 cup butter (margarine)

3 tablespoons cocoa

6 tablespoons milk

2 eggs

1 box powdered sugar

1 cups nuts

1 teaspoon vanilla

Preparation

In a saucepan bring butter, cocoa, and milk to a boil. Remove from fire. Add powdered sugar, nuts, and vanilla. Mix. Spread over hot cake as soon it's out of the oven.

My Two Cents

Many families have a "chocolate cake" recipe that they love. In Texas, some fancy in Texas Sheet Cake. My family has what we all call "Grandma Cake" and it has its roots in our Alabama, Oklahoma, Buttermilk lends a taste and texture to baking that is so good. I used to try to make buttermilk by adding vinegar or lemon to milk. The great thing about this flavor is that your result is a smooth, rich cake that is not TOO sweet. I now believe that it is worth the effort to purchase a quart of the "good stuff" to bring out the flavor of baking. My grandmother made this cake, and it was my favorite. She made this for me for my birthday, and it was the best gift ever.

2 C sugar   1/2 c shortening

2 egg, unbeaten   1 1/2 c. buttermilk

2 C flour

2 T cocoa   dash of salt

1 tsp vanilla   1 tsp soda

1 c. boiling water

Cream shortening & sugar. Add eggs & beat. Combine dry ingredients & add alternately with buttermilk. Add vanilla. Combine boiling water & soda. Add last. Bake 350° in large loaf pan. 45 mins, until well done.

14. Creole Cake-Original

There are a few different types of cake referred to as "Creole Cake" this is my grandma's version and hard to beat.

Intermediate   60-Minutes

Ingredients

2 cup sugar

2 eggs, unbeaten

2 cups flour

2 tablespoon cocoa

a dash of salt

1 teaspoon soda

1 teaspoon vanilla

1 cup boiling water

1/2 cup shortening

1/2 cup buttermilk

Preparation

Cream shortening and sugar, add eggs and beat. Combine dry ingredients and add alternately with buttermilk, add vanilla. Combine boiling water and soda. Add last. Bake at 350 degrees in a large loaf pan for 45 minutes until well done.

Icing

1 c. brown sugar

½ cup evaporated milk

¾ cube oleo

1 c nuts

Pour over cake & put under broiler.

Good!

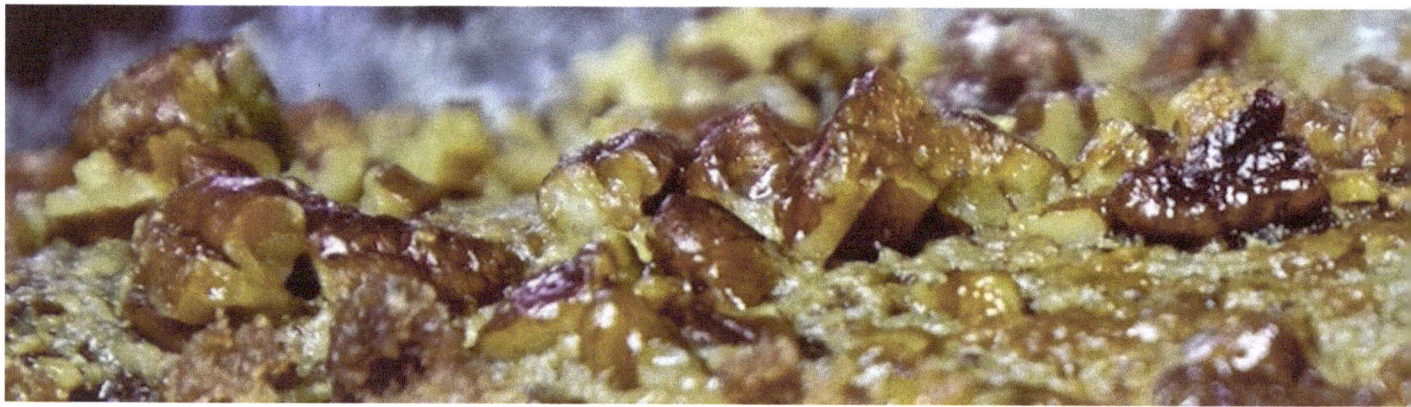

14 b. Creole Cake Broiled Icing-Buttery

This icing is buttery and nutty and adds a beautiful texture to this tasty Creole cake.

 Easy

 20-Minutes

Ingredients

1 cup brown sugar

1/2 cup evaporated milk

3/4 stick (6 tablespoons) of butter (margarine)

1 cup nuts

Preparation

Pour over cake and put under the broiler until it browns.

My Two Cents

There are a few variations that I have seen that are called "Creole Cake" but they all refer to a nutty filling. Brown sugar, butter, and nuts bring out a whole new flavor and texture to the chocolate version. You will find that your guests will be impressed by your original down-home recipe.

NOTES:

_____
_____
_____
_____
_____
_____

1 1/2 c sugar   2 c Fruit Cocktail
2 eggs   2 c flour
                       2 T soda (teaspoons)
                       1/2 tsp salt

Pour into greased loaf pan, Sprinkle
with 1 c nuts & 1 1/2 brown sugar
Bake 40 - 45 mins . 325°

Topping

Boil 3/4 c sugar + 1/3 c. margarine

1/2 c evaporated milk
1 tsp vanilla
    Boil 2 min . Pour over
    hot cake.

15. Fruit Cocktail Cake-Old Fashioned

What a fabulous old-time traditional cake that will bring back memories for those who enjoy this fruity treat.

 Easy

 90-Minutes

Ingredients

CAKE

1 1/2 cups sugar

2 eggs

2 cups fruit cocktail

2 cups flour

2 teaspoons soda

1/2 teaspoon salt

1 cup nuts (sprinkle top)

1/2 cup brown sugar

TOPPING

3/4 cup sugar

1/3 cup margarine

1/2 cup evaporated milk

1 teaspoon vanilla

Preparation

CAKE

Pour into greased loaf pan. Sprinkle with nuts and brown sugar. Bake 40-45 minutes at 325 degrees.

TOPPING

Boil sugar, butter and evaporated milk, vanilla for 2 minutes. Pour over hot cake.

My Two Cents

When you add something like fruit cocktail to a cake, you get a tender, moist cake. This cake has no oil, but the texture is terrific. The boiled topping gives just the right amount of buttery taste to the cake sealing in the richness and bold flavor.

Fruit Cocktail
Cake

1 pkg (4 oz.) Baker's German Sweet Chocolate
1/2 c boiling water
2 1/4 C. sifted flour
1 tsp baking soda
1/2 tsp salt
1 c butter or margaine   1 c buttermilk
2 c sugar   4 egg whites
4 egg yolks   (stiffly beaten)
1 tsp vanilla   Frosting

Melt chocolate in boiling water, cool.
Sift flour, soda + salt. Cream butter +
sugar well. Add egg yolks, one at a time,
beating after each. Fold in egg whites, beaten.
Pour into 3 9" layer pans, greased +
floured. Bake 350° 30-35 min. Cool.
     Spread with frosting. Frost
     between layers.

Coconut-Pecan Frosting
     Combine 1 c evaporated milk, 1 c sugar,
3 egg yolks, 1/2 C. butter or margarine +
1 tsp vanilla in saucepan. Cook over
medium heat, stirring constantly until Cool.
mixture thickens. Remove + add 1 1/3 c coconut 1 c
                                          pecans

16. German Chocolate Cake-Authentic

My dad loved this cake, and we often made it for his birthday and other occasions. The German Chocolate lends a unique flavor to this old-school delight.

Intermediate

60-Minutes

Ingredients

1 package (4oz.) Bakers German Sweet Chocolate

1/2 cup boiling water

2 1/4 cups sifted flour

1 teaspoon baking soda

1/2 teaspoon salt

1 cup margarine

2 cups sugar

4 egg yolks

1 teaspoon vanilla

1 cup buttermilk

4 egg whites (stiffly beaten)

Preparation

Melt chocolate in boiling water, cool. Sift flour, soda, and salt. Cream butter and sugar well. Add egg yolks, one at a time beating after each. Fold in egg whites, beaten. Pour into 3, 9 inch prepared layer cake pans (greased and floured.) Bake at 350 degrees for 30-35 minutes. Cool. Spread with frosting. Frost between layers.

Frosting

1 cup evaporated milk

1 cup sugar

3 egg yolks

1/2 cup butter (margarine)

1 teaspoon vanilla

1 1/3 cups coconut

1 cup pecans

Preparation

In a saucepan combine evaporated milk, sugar, egg yolks, butter and vanilla. Cook over medium heat constantly stirring until mixture it thickens. Remove and add coconut and pecans.

2 c sugar

1 c. cooking oil

3 eggs

2 small jars red plum babyfood

2 c all purpose flour

1/2 t. baking soda

1/2 t salt

1 t cinnamon

1 t. ground cloves

1 c. chopped pecans

Cream together sugar, oil & eggs. Add plums & mix thoroughly.

Combine flour, soda, salt & cinnamon and cloves. Add to creamed mixture & blend well.

Bake in a tube pan for 1 hour. 350°
Cool in pan for 10 mins.

Puncture top of cake with tines of fork so topping will soak in.

Topping

1 c. powdered sugar

2 T Lemon juice

Barely bring to a boil. Pour over cake while still warm.

17. Red Plum Cake-Delightful

What a fabulous old-time traditional cake that will bring back memories for those who enjoy this fruity treat.

 Easy

 90-Minutes

Ingredients

2 cups sugar

1 cup cooking oil

3 eggs

2 small jars red plum baby food (or

cook down 2 red plums and a 1/2

cup sugar in the microwave)

2 cup all-purpose flour

1/2 teaspoon baking soda

1/2 teaspoon salt

1 teaspoon cinnamon

1 teaspoon ground cloves

1 cup chopped pecans

GLAZE

1 cup powdered sugar

2 tablespoons lemon juice

Preparation

CAKE

Cream together sugar, oil, and eggs Add plums and mix thoroughly. Combine flour, soda, salt, cinnamon, and cloves. Add to creamed mixture and blend well. Bake in a tube pan for 1 hour at 350 degrees. Cool in pan for 10 minutes. Puncture top of cake with tines of fork so topping will soak in.

TOPPING

Barely bring to a boil. Pour over cake while still warm.

My Two Cents

The use of baby food makes the texture quite moist. The topping adds a unique touch to this sweet specialty. This cake is rich and moist. I love fresh ingredients and used 2 fresh red plums and added 1/4-1/2 cup sugar cooking them down via the microwave till soft. Take off skin and pit then stir.

1½ c sugar
2 c oil
2 egg beaten
1 tsp. vinegar
2 oz Red food Coloring
2½ c. flour
1 tsp soda
1 tsp salt
2 T. cocoa
1 C buttermilk   1 tsp vanilla

Cream sugar + oil together in a
mixing bowl. Add eggs, beat well, add
vinegar + food coloring. Beat well.
Sift flour, soda, salt + cocoa
together + add to cream mixture
Cream mixture alternately with buttermilk
+ vanilla. Beat well.
Bake in 2 9" greased pans, floured at
350° for 30 - 35 min.
Frost with Buttercream frosting.

54

18. Red Velvet Cake-Sinful

My very first boyfriend's mom made this cake for him as it was his favorite. I still remember the smooth texture and how it melts in one's mouth. His mom was born and raised in Virginia and comes from a long line of traditional southern cooks.

 Easy

 30-Minutes

Ingredients

- 1/2 cup sugar
- 2 cups oil
- 2 eggs beaten
- teaspoon vinegar
- 2 oz. red food coloring
- 2 1/2 cups flour
- teaspoon soda
- teaspoon salt
- 2 tablespoons cocoa
- cup buttermilk
- teaspoon vanilla

Preparation

Cream sugar and oil together in a mixing bowl. Add eggs, beat well, add vinegar and food coloring. Beat well. Sift flour, soda, salt, and cocoa together adding them to the cream mixture. Cream mixture alternately with buttermilk and vanilla. Beat well. Bake in 2, 9" greased pans (floured) at 350 degrees for 30-35 minutes. Frost with Buttercream frosting.

My Two Cents

You will fall in love with this original version of this cake. It has found itself in a revival over the past ten years. You can see some "Red Velvet" cookies, cakes or cupcakes on the menu at most bakeries currently. My first boyfriend's mother was born in VA and lived in TN when I asked her for her recipe for his favorite cake. It has served me well throughout time, but I think you will find less moist and dense cakes currently being made. I enjoy the not too sweet aspect of this traditional southern specialty.

Melt 1 stick margarine in the bottom of a large pan. Sift together 1 C flour, 1 C sugar, 2 tsp. vanilla. Stir into batter. add 1 cup milk Pour batter over melted margarine in pans. Then arrange canned peaches over this. Sprinkle 1/4 C. sugar & 3/4 tsp cinnamon over top Bake 350° for 1 hour. Can substitute other fruit.

19. Fruit Cobbler–Crispy

One of my most favorite sweets is a cobbler. I remember as a girl in school the cafeteria lady made an excellent "Apple Crisp" and I couldn't wait for lunch when it was on the menu. Later in life, I moved to Oklahoma where my grandma lived and find myself significantly influenced by her rendition of cobbler. Fast and easy this recipe is a sure win.

 Easy

 90-Minutes

Ingredients

stick (1/2 cup) of butter
(margarine)

cup flour

cup sugar

cup milk

teaspoons vanilla

can peaches, blueberries or the
fruit of your choice. (Cook down
he frozen or fresh fruit.)

/2 teaspoon salt

teaspoons baking powder

OP

/4 cup sugar

/4 teaspoon sugar

Preparation

Melt one stick margarine in the bottom of a large pan. Sift together flour, sugar, vanilla and milk stir into a batter. Pour batter over melted butter (margarine) in pans. Then arrange canned peaches over this.
Sprinkle sugar and cinnamon over the top. Bake at 350 degrees for 1 hour.
Can substitute with other fruit.

My Two Cents

A cobbler that has a generous amount of juice is one of my all-time favorite desserts to eat and make. My family has many cobbler makers that have historically enjoyed improvising to include the "seasonal fruit" that might be available.

NOTES:

_____

2 c brown sugar
1 c margarine
1/2 c corn syrup
1 tsp salt
1 tsp soda
1 tsp butter
6 qt. popped corn, Peanuts

Combine brown sugar, margarine, syrup & salt. Bring to a boil. Boil for 5 minutes. Remove from heat. Add soda & butter. Pour over popped corn & nutmeats. Toss gently. Spread on a cookie sheet. Place in a preheated 200° oven for 1 hour stirring every 15 minutes. Remove from oven, Cool. Store in a covered container.

Makes 6 quarts.

20. Oven Caramel Corn-Gooey

My mom loved to make this as the crunch on the inside and gooeyness on the outside is just unbeatable. So yummy you might want to double your recipe so you can have enough for everyone.

 Easy

 90-Minutes

Ingredients

2 cups brown sugar

1 cup margarine

1/2 cup corn syrup

1 teaspoon salt

1 teaspoon soda

1 teaspoon butter

6 quarts popped corn

1/2 cup peanuts (optional)

Preparation

Combine brown sugar, margarine (butter), syrup and salt. Bring to a boil. Boil for 5 minutes. Remove from heat. Add soda and butter. Pour over popped corn and nut meats. Toss gently. Spread on a cookie sheet. Place in a preheated 200-degree oven for one-hour stirring every 15 minutes. Remove from oven, cool. Store in a covered container. Makes six quarts.

My Two Cents

Try a homemade gooey treat that everyone on your list will love. You will be inspired to make holiday wreaths, fill bins with Caramel Corn or make popcorn balls that you can decorate and give as gifts. I love this traditional sweet that is popular in many homes across America. You will master this oven version of a sweet and salty snack. Those on your gift list will love you for taking the extra time and effort to make this for them. Follow the directions precisely and measure carefully to ensure success.

Caramel Corn

4 c Sugar
1 lg. can evaporated milk
1 cube butter.
Bring to soft **Ball** stage.
Take from fire — add 7 oz jar of
marshallow cream, 2 pkgs. of
Chocolate chips. Stir until disolved
then add 2 c nuts. Pour into
buttered cookie sheet. Cool.
Put in Refrigerator.

21. Marshmallow Fudge-Fast

Simple, scrumptious and satisfying is what you will say once you make your first batch of this excellent fudge.

 Easy

 90-Minutes

Ingredients

4 cups sugar

1 large can evaporated-milk

1/2 cup butter

7-ounce jar of marshmallow cream

2 packages of chocolate chips

2 cups nuts

Preparation

In a saucepan cook sugar, evaporated milk and butter to soft ball stage. Take mixture from fire and add marshmallow cream and chocolate chips stirring until dissolved then add nuts. Pour into buttered cookie sheet. Cool. Put in refrigerator.

My Two Cents

I have historically had issues with soft ball and hard ball sugar stages and how to read them. I suggest you learn how to test the stages of sugar when making candy. You have here a pretty easy recipe because it uses marshmallow cream and evaporated milk to help with consistency.

NOTES:

_____

_____

_____

2 c. Sugar
dash of salt
3 T cocoa
1 sm can Carnation milk
    Cook until forms a
firm ball stirring constantly.
    Add 1 C pecans
2 tsp vanilla
2 T butter & peanut butter
Stir until it loses its gloss. Drop

by spoonfuls onto wax paper or
pour into pan

    Sheri — even you can't
fail with this candy.
        Love you —
            Mom!

22. No-Fail Fudge-Fantastic

Historically I fail to make fudge the right consistency. I either over or under cook it most every time. Even in the making of this cookbook when I made this fudge for the FIRST time I "FAILED" which was pretty ironic. It is pretty simple if you pay attention to the temperature and use a thermometer if you don't know how to test for a "firm ball" stage. Delicious.

 Easy

 20-Minutes

Ingredients

2 cups sugar

a dash of salt

3 tablespoons cocoa

1 small can carnation milk

1 cup pecans

2 teaspoons vanilla

2 tablespoons butter or peanut butter

Preparation

In a saucepan cook to firm ball stage stirring constantly. Add pecans, vanilla, butter (or peanut butter.) Stir until it loses it gloss. Drop by spoonfuls onto wax paper or pour into pan.

My Two Cents

It is a great accomplishment to make perfect fudge. I have trouble cooking it to the right soft or firm ball stage and tend to over or under cook it. Practice makes perfect, so try a couple of times before the holidays, so you have it down and won't have a fudge fail issue when serving your family and friends.

No-Fail Fudge

2 c sugar
1 tsp. soda
1 c. buttermilk
3/4 c butter or margarine
1 tsp. vanilla
2 c Pecans chopped

Combine all ingredients except vanilla + pecans in 4 1/2 quart glass bowl, mix well. Microwave on Roast (High) for 15 minutes, mix well. Microwave on roast for 13-15 minutes longer to soft ball stage or 236° on candy thermometer. Stir in vanilla. Beat until soft peaks form. Stir in pecans. Spread in 9 x 12 in. baking dish. Cool. Cut into squares.

23. Oklahoma Brown-Microwave Version

What a unique flavor you will find in this "browned sugar" based candy AKA Aunt Bill's Brown Candy very original. The regular version calls for a cast iron skillet and requires a great deal more labor that our microwave recipe.

Intermediate   90-Minutes

Ingredients

cups sugar

teaspoon soda

cup buttermilk

3/4 cups butter or margarine

teaspoon vanilla

cups pecans (chopped)

Preparation

Combine all ingredients except vanilla and pecans in 4 1/2-quart glass bowl, mix well. Microwave on Roast (high) for 15 minutes, mix well. Microwave on roast for 13-15 min (I cooked mine for 10 min or so in a modern microwave as this was recipe written 30 years ago. In those days technology did not allow us to produce as high watt microwaves as today. Use your candy thermometer) or longer to soft ball stage or 236 degrees on a candy thermometer. Stir in vanilla. Beat until soft peaks form. Stir in pecans. Spread in 7x12 inch baking dish. Cool. Cut into squares.

My Two Cents

As the invention of the microwave demanded, recipes for those that preferred to use this method to cook needed to convert original recipes. "Oklahoma Brown" is what my dad called this candy that my great grandma from Oklahoma made with her sister and mailed it to us in Michigan.

Oklahoma
Brown

2 C Sugar   1/2 c water
1 tsp Salt   2 T Margarine or butter
1 C White Syrup   1 tsp vanilla
2 C. peanuts   2 tsp soda

Boil sugar, syrup & water in large pan until it spins a thread (235°). Add peanuts & cook until slightly brown. 280°. Turn off flame & add butter, salt & vanilla & soda last. Stir slightly, until candy foams & soda is well mixed! Pour on greased pan. Do Not Over mix or cAndy will be Tough.

Let cool & break into pieces.

24. Peanut Brittle-Sweet

What a treat it is to have homemade peanut brittle to add to your gift baskets or to place on your table.

Intermediate   20-Minutes

Ingredients

2 cups sugar

1 teaspoon salt

1 cup white syrup

2 cups peanuts

1/2 cup water

2 tablespoons butter (margarine)

1 teaspoon vanilla

2 teaspoons soda

Preparation

Boil sugar, syrup, and water in a large pan until it spins a thread (235 degrees.) Add peanuts and cook until slightly brown (280 degrees.) Turn off the flame and add butter, salt, vanilla and soda last. Stir slightly, until candy foams and soda is well mixed. Pour into a greased pan. DO NOT OVER MIX or candy will be tough. Let cool and break into pieces.

My Two Cents

Such an elegant added touch to any table or goody tray. This candy is such a yummy and delicious treat. Take extra care in making this. Pay particular attention to timing and the temperature at which you cook the ingredients. Use a thermometer to assist you in determining arrival at the stage where it "spins a thread." Just take your time, and you will enjoy giving this as gifts to those special folks in your life.

Peanut Brittle

1 C Karo
1 C Sugar
Heat to boiling
Add 1½ C Peanut Butter
Add 4 C Special K or
- Rice Krispies
1 tsp Vanilla

25. Cereal Peanut Butter Candy-Dreamy

Every time I make this I get requests for the recipe. The recipe is easy to make if you remember that as soon as it reaches a full boil take it off the fire and add the rest of your ingredients. The cereals I recommend are corn flakes, Special K or rice crispies.

Intermediate   30-Minutes

Ingredients

- cup white syrup
- cup sugar
- 1/2 cup peanut butter
- cups cereal (rice or flakes)
- teaspoon vanilla

Preparation

Heat white syrup and sugar just to a full boil then add peanut butter. Finally, add cereal and vanilla.

My Two Cents

Here is a spin on the rice cereal treats that we know and love. Decorate with food coloring for a spectacular presentation for your guests and gift baskets. Your family may not be able to wait until a special occasion to enjoy this candy, so teach many family members how to make this anytime.

NOTES:

_____

_____

_____

_____

_____

_____

2 c sugar
1 c buttermilk
1 tsp soda
1/8 tsp salt
Cook together over high heat for
5-6 minutes. Add: 2 T butter +
1-2 1/2 c. pecans. Cook 5 - 6
minutes on high heat. Take off fire,
will be foaming. Beat down foam.
Beat until dropping consistancy, Hurry Up!

26. Pecan Pralines-Southern

I channel my aunt's candy making talent when I make these pralines. They are morsels of caramelized sugar complemented by the nuttiness of pecans. Using a thermometer ensures cooking it to the right temperature thus the texture will be perfect.

 Intermediate    30-Minutes

Ingredients

2 cups sugar

1 cup buttermilk

1 teaspoon soda

1/8 teaspoon salt

2 tablespoons butter

1-2 1/2 cups pecans

Preparation

Cook sugar, buttermilk, soda, and salt together over high heat for 5-6 minutes then add butter and pecans. Cook 5-6 minutes on high heat. Take off the fire. The mixture will be foaming. Beat down the foam. Beat until dropping consistency. Hurry Up!

My Two Cents

Nothing better than freshly made pecan pralines. What a rare treat for your loved ones! You certainly want to pass along how to make this recipe. Practice making this type of candy. You will be asked to make many batches once people eat this treat.

NOTES:

_____

_____

3/4 c sugar	1 pkg 8 oz dates
2 eggs	1 tsp vanilla
1 cube margarine	1 c pecans

Mix all these ingredients & cook over low flame for 10 minutes. Take off fire & cool for a few seconds. Add 3 c. Rice Krispies. Make balls & roll in powdered sugar or

Coconut. Delicious!

Cookies

27. Date Cookies-Hearty

Dates bring a tangy flare to this recipe. The rice crispies make it so easy to create these balls that are held together by moist dates, butter, and eggs. Pecans are the perfect addition to this cookie.

 Easy

 30-Minutes

Ingredients

3/4 cup sugar

2 eggs

1 cube (1/2 cup or stick) butter or margarine

1 package (8 oz) dates

1 teaspoon vanilla

1 cup pecans

3 cups rice crispies

Preparation

Mix all of these ingredients and cook over low flame for 10 minutes. Take off the fire and cool for a few seconds. Add 3 cups rice crispy cereal. Make balls and roll in powdered sugar or coconut. Delicious!

My Two Cents

I make these yummy cookies during the holidays. This no-bake cookie is a treat that many will enjoy at your next family dinner or dressed up as "holiday fare."

NOTES:

_____

_____

_____

_____

_____

2½ C Sugar
1 C Evaporated milk
1 pkg chopped Dates
2 C nuts

Boil sugar + milk to soft ball stage. Add dates + cook until dates soften. Add nuts + cool after adding 2 T butter & 1 tsp vanilla. Pour on a damp cheesecloth + roll into a round roll. Slice.

28. Date Roll-Nuggetty

People will rave about these when you make them due to the heartiness, flavor, and appearance.

 Easy

 30-Minutes

Ingredients

2 1/2 cups sugar

1 cup evaporated milk

1-pound package chopped dates

2 cups nuts

2 tablespoons butter (margarine)

1 teaspoon vanilla

Preparation

Boil sugar and mil to soft ball stage. Add nuts and cool after adding butter and vanilla. Pour on a damp cheesecloth and roll into a round roll. Slice.

My Two Cents

What an excellent old-fashioned treat this roll is. This date roll is moist, and you will find that it makes a big hit at the holidays or any day. Be sure to add this to your goodie trays for the holidays, and people will rave at the way you integrate old and new tastes.

NOTES:

_____

_____

_____

_____

_____

_____

3/4 c shortening   1/2 c molasses
1 c sugar   2 c sifted flour
1 egg   1/4 tsp salt
        2 tsp soda
        1 tsp ginger
        1 tsp cinnamon   Combine
        1 tsp nutmeg

Chill 1 hour, Roll into balls,
Roll in sugar, Bake 350°. Makes
6 doz. cookies.

29. Ginger Snaps–Tasty

I can smell these baking in my grandma's house. Such a potent combination of ginger and molasses that brings back so many memories.

 Easy

 30-Minutes

Ingredients

3/4 cup shortening

1 cup sugar

1 egg

1/2 cup molasses

2 cups sifted flour

1/4 teaspoon salt

2 teaspoons soda

1 teaspoon ginger

1 teaspoon cinnamon

1 teaspoon nutmeg

Preparation

Chill for one hour. Roll into balls, Roll in sugar. Bake at 350 degrees. Makes 6 dozen cookies.

My Two Cents

A distinctive taste floods your mouth as you bite into this cookie and "snap" a bite. The rich flavor and aroma are one of a kind. The dark color adds a unique touch to your gift boxes, tins, and special occasion trays. I love these and believe you can't beat this homemade version founded back as early as the Colonists in America.

NOTES:

_____

_____

_____

_____

_____

1 c. shortening
3/4 c brown sugar (Packet)
3/4 c. granulated sugar

1 egg   1 tsp. salt
1 tsp vanilla   1/2 tsp. baking soda
3 1/4 c. oats   1/2 tsp cinnamon
1/4 c water
1 c. flour

Cream shortening + sugars.

Beat in egg, vanilla, oatmeal + water.

Sift flour, salt, soda + cinnamon + stir into ~~greased~~ ~~cookie~~ sugar mixture. Drop by teaspoonfuls onto greased cookie sheet. Bake 15 minutes 350° degrees. 5 Dozen

30. Oatmeal Cookies (Chewy)–Soft

Growing up my mom made these a great deal for me, and I once again am taken back to a happy time with every bite when I make these chewy delights.

 Easy

 30-Minutes

Ingredients

1 cup shortening

3/4 cup brown sugar (packed)

3/4 cup granulated sugar

1 egg

1 teaspoon vanilla

3 1/4 cups oats

1/4 cup water

1 cup flour

1 teaspoon salt

1/2 teaspoon baking soda

1/2 teaspoon cinnamon

Preparation

Cream shortening and sugars. Beat in egg, vanilla, oatmeal, and water. Sift flour, salt, soda and cinnamon and stir into sugar mixture. Add raisins, cranberries, or nuts (optional.) Drop by teaspoonfuls onto a greased cookie sheet. Bake 15 minutes at 350 degrees. Makes 5 dozen cookies.

My Two Cents

I like a "chewy" oatmeal cookie. The texture of this cookie is the ticket that will make your family and friends sneak a second and third cookie. Line your holiday tins with these healthy treats. Oatmeal helps lower cholesterol and are an excellent source of fiber. Your variations and creativity will add a new touch to an old-school delight. In the American South and Midwest, oats have been a crop that fed horses, kids, young and old. Fruit is a staple that we find in cookies, bars, fruit crisps and so much more. Reconnect with a wholesome and satisfying source of nutrition.

4 T. Cocoa
1/2 c. Milk
2 c Sugar
1 cube margarine
   Boil 2 minutes.

Add 1 c Peanut Butter, 3 c oatmeal
1 c nuts. Form small cookies,
Cool.

31. No-Bake Cookies-Yummy

The blend of peanut butter and chocolate along with the oats make this no-bake cookie one you will find yourself making a great deal.

 Easy

 20-Minutes

Ingredients

4 tablespoons cocoa

1/2 cup milk

2 cups sugar

1 cube (1/2 cup butter or margarine)

1 cup peanut butter

3 cups oatmeal

1 cup nuts (optional)

Preparation

Boil cocoa, milk, sugar and butter (margarine) for two minutes. Add the peanut butter, oatmeal, and nuts (optional.) Form small cookies. Cool.

My Two Cents

This recipe is for one of my favorite cookies and so excellent. I love making these for any occasion. Friends and family won't be able to get enough of these treats so double your batch. Keep one for your loved ones and one for holiday gifts. Enjoy! Keep an eye on the boiling time as it is a crucial component to making the consistency perfect.

NOTES:

_____

_____

_____

_____

_____

1 pkg. spice cake mix
1/4 c water
1 c oatmeal
1/4 c oil
2 eggs
1 c raisins

Combine all. Drop by large teaspoonfuls onto greased cookie sheet Bake 425° - 10 minutes until light brown.

32. Oatmeal Cookies (Spicy)–Quick

These are fast and easy when you need a recipe to make with a grandchild or just for a goodie for afternoon tea.

 Easy

 20-Minutes

Ingredients

1 package spice cake mix

1/4 cup water

1 cup oatmeal

1/4 cup oil

2 eggs

1 cup raisins

Preparation

Combine all. Drop by large teaspoonfuls onto greased cookie sheet. Back 425 degrees for 10 minutes until light brown.

My Two Cents

My mom liked shortcuts. They were a welcomed change to someone who baked from scratch. She loved to use mixes to compliment age-old recipes and simplify the process. As "cake mixes" became famous in her young adulthood; she created this cookie which is easy to make.

NOTES:

_____

_____

_____

_____

_____

_____

1 c shortening
1/8 lb. of butter (1/2 cube)
1 1/2 c sugar
2 eggs
2 3/4 c flour
2 tsp Cream of Tartar
1 tsp soda
1/4 tsp salt
Cream sugar, butter & shortening,

add eggs & dry ingredients. Roll
into balls about size of Walnuts.
Roll in sugar & cinnamon.
Bake 375°. About 10 mins.

33. Snickerdoodle Cookies-Fabulous Flavor

These cookies give new meaning to the words soft and flaky as there is nothing quite like them. Cinnamon lovers will revel in the aroma as they wait for the first one out of the oven.

 Easy

 30-Minutes

Ingredients

1 cup shortening

1/8 pound of butter (1/2 cube or stick)

1 1/2 cups sugar

2 eggs

2 3/4 cups flour

2 teaspoons Cream of Tartar

1 teaspoon soda

1/4 teaspoon salt

Preparation

Cream sugar, butter, and shortening. Add eggs and dry ingredients. Roll into balls the size of walnuts. Roll in sugar and cinnamon. Bake at 375 degrees for 10 minutes.

My Two Cents

I love this cookie which has quickly has become my new "go to" recipe. I appreciate the simplicity and great taste. It is a nice change since I tend to make chocolate chip or sugar cookies more regularly. I love the unique flakiness and touch of cinnamon. The outside has a crunch, and the inside is so light with its buttery taste. You will find yourself making this cookie quite often. Share this and other recipes with family and friends. Watch this become one you see when you get baked goods from others you have inspired.

1/2 C margarine
1 C sugar
2 eggs
2 T cream   Chill.
1 tsp vanilla   Roll on floured
2 1/2 C. flour   Board - Cut.
1/2 tsp salt   Bake. 375° til
1/4 tsp soda - light Brown (firm)

34. Sugar Cookie (Basic)-Authentic

Who doesn't like a good sugar cookie? Creative decorating makes these so much fun to make so invite friends and family to gather together and have a blast.

 Easy

 30-Minutes

Ingredients

1/2 cup butter (margarine)

1 cup sugar

2 eggs

2 tablespoons cream

1 teaspoon vanilla

2 1/2 cups flour

1/2 teaspoon salt

1/4 teaspoon soda

Preparation

Chill. Roll on floured board. Cut. Bake at 375 degrees until light brown (firm.)

My Two Cents

The sky is the limit when you use a basic sugar cookie dough. The kids love to make these and cut them out with their favorite cookie cutters. If you frost them or merely sprinkle sugar on them, they are going to be a hit.

NOTES:

_____

_____

_____

_____

_____

_____

_____

Mix 1 c. shortening
   1/2 c sugar
   1/2 c brown sugar
   2 eggs
Sift together & stir in
   2 3/4 c flour
   1/2 tsp soda
   1 tsp salt
2 tsp cinnamon or 1 tsp vanilla

Mix with hands. Press &
mold into a long, smooth
roll.

Wrap in wax paper & chill
until stiff. Cut thin

Bake on ungreased sheet
until slightly brown. 400°

35. Sugar Cookies (Refrigerator)-Crumbly

Growing up my mom made these a great deal for me, and I once again am taken back to a happy time with every bite when I make these chewy delights.

 Easy

 30-Minutes

Ingredients

1 cup shortening

1/2 cup sugar

1/2 cup brown sugar

2 eggs

2 3/4 cups flour

1/2 teaspoon soda

1 teaspoon salt

2 teaspoons cinnamon OR

1 teaspoon vanilla

Preparation

Mix with hands. Press and mold into a long, smooth roll. Wrap in wax paper and chill until stiff. Cut thin. Bake on ungreased cookie sheet until slightly brown at 400 degrees.

My Two Cents

Refrigerator cookies are great because you can cut them all at once or a slice at a time. Explore all the possible designs you will make alongside your family members and friends as you share this experience together.

NOTES:

_____
_____
_____
_____
_____

2/3 portion Corn bread to
1/3 portion white bread (dryed + cubed.)
1 can mushroom soup
3 eggs
1 c chopped onion   cook w
1 c celery   1/4 (1 cube) butter
Add onion + celery to bread crumbs mixing together with Chicken broth. Season to taste with Poultry seasoning.

Dressing and Savory Pudding
36. Cornbread Dressing-Old Time

My great grandma used to make this. She was on the rolls of the Chickasaw Tribe and also has American Pioneer ancestors. The flavor of the newly established Territory comes through in this recipe.

 Easy

 90-Minutes

Ingredients

2/3 portion cornbread

1/3 portion white bread (dried and cubed)

1 can mushroom soup

3 eggs

1 cup chopped onion

1 cup celery

1 can chicken broth (until moist)

1/4 cube of butter

Preparation

Add onion and celery (cook in butter) to breadcrumbs mixing together with chicken broth. Season to taste with poultry seasoning.

My Two Cents

To me, there has never been any question of what type of dressing to make with poultry. This dressing compliments the taste of a bird with the flavors of onion and celery. The mushroom soup holds it together. The chicken broth ensures the mixture stays moist. My daughter likes to change it up veering off from our family favorite by adding cranberries. I can't wait to go to the refrigerator to dish up a heap of dressing to go with my leftovers. I love to have chicken broth on hand to moisten the leftover dressing. Be sure to make plenty of this dressing. It is so amazing that family and friends will want seconds and thirds.

3 egg
1 T grated onion
2 T sugar
1 tsp salt
3 T flour
2 T melted butter
1 can (16 oz) creamed corn.
2 c milk (scalded)
   (Good if you add an additional
drained whole kernel corn.
   pour into casserole.

   Bake 325 — 50 min's.

37. Corn Pudding-Custardy

The unique taste and texture will have your family and friends talking about this side for a long time.

 Easy

 90-Minutes

Ingredients

3 eggs

1 tablespoon grated onion

2 tablespoons sugar

1 teaspoon salt

3 tablespoons flour

2 tablespoons melted butter

1 can (16 ounces) creamed corn

1 can (drained) whole kernel corn (optional)

2 cup milk (Scalded)

Preparation

If you like, corn you can try adding an extra can of drained whole kernel corn. Pour into casserole. Bake 325 for 50 minutes.

My Two Cents

A southern favorite that is beyond compare and is very rich and delicious. The eggs make this light and fluffy, reminiscent of a soufflé. Once again you will be the hit of the party, dinner or just an ordinary evening meal. Satisfying and scrumptious.

NOTES:

_____

_____

_____

_____

_____

_____

Peel + core 6-8 large delicious apples
slice apples in bowl.
Mix in 1 t Cinnamon
1/2 tsp salt , toss with 2 tablespoons flour
8-10 pkge artificial Sweetner, OR 3/4 cup sugar
Pour into pie crust. Cover with top.
Dot with 1 T Butter.

Pie Crust
2 c flour, 1 tsp salt

2/3 c crisco
6 T cold water
Blend flour + crisco . Add as
much water as you need to keep
dough together . Don't handle
dough a lot or it gets tough . Roll
on floured Board.
Makes 2 crust.

Pies

38. Apple Pie (Sugar Free) and Crust-Awesome

Since my mom was a diabetic, she always searched for good recipes that were sugar-free. It was quite tricky back in the day when artificial sweeteners tasted...well...artificial. This beautiful pie is delightful with sugar or a replacement.

 Easy

 90-Minutes

Ingredients

Peel and core 6-8 large red delicious apples (try Honeycrisp) and slice apples in a bowl.

Mix in 1 tablespoon cinnamon

1/2 teaspoon salt

2 tablespoons flour

8-10 packages artificial sweetener (or 3/4 cup sugar)

1/2 teaspoon ground cloves

1 tablespoon butter

CRUST

2 cups flour

1 teaspoon salt

2/3 cup shortening

6 tablespoons cold water

Preparation

Mix in 1 tablespoon cinnamon, teaspoon salt, artificial sweetener. Pour into pie crust. Cover with top crust. Dot with 1 tablespoon butter.

CRUST

Blend flour and shortening. Add as much water necessary to keep the dough together. Don't handle dough a lot or it gets tough. Roll on floured board. Makes two crusts.

My Two Cents

My mother lived a short life due to diabetes. As a result of this disease, she always looked for ways to make "sugar-free" baked goods. She loved to create goodies and eat them too. She mastered this apple pie, and I am happy to share this with you. The pie crust is best when made with cold water to help ensure the flakiness. It is simple. After one taste of a pie with the crust she has here, you will never again purchase a frozen crust. I have grown to love "Honeycrisp" apples and recommend them as they are so sweet, crisp and juicy.

Apple Pie

Pie Crust

1/2 c Butter
2 c Sugar
2 T Cornstarch
Add 4 eggs one at a time. Beat
mixture well each time. Pinch of salt
Vanilla 1 tsp, if desired. Pour into
unbaked pie shell.
Bake 4 or 5 minutes at 450°
reduce to 350 for about 35 min. Check
with knife.

39. Cheese Pie-Simple

When you only have a few essential ingredients you can still make a great pie. Many Sunday afternoons have been spent in the south over a "cup of Joe" and a piece of Cheese Pie. Sweet, simple to make a so good.

 Easy

 45-Minutes

Ingredients

1/2 cup butter

2 cups sugar

2 tablespoons cornstarch

4 eggs add one at a time

1 pinch of salt

2 eggs

1 teaspoon vanilla, if desired

3 tablespoons unsweetened cocoa
(optional for a chocolate variation)

Preparation

Beat the mixture well each time. Pour into an unbaked pie shell. Bake 4 to 5 minutes at 450 degrees. Reduce to 350 degrees for about 35 minutes. Check for doneness with a knife.

My Two Cents

Do you love cheesecake? Then you will enjoy this type of dessert. You may feel like adding berries of red, white and blue on top of this easy to make kind of pie. The sky is the limit to the way you can serve this. What a great compliment to a cup of tea or coffee this pie is. You will "wow" your friends and neighbors with your scratch version of cheese pie.

NOTES:

_____

_____

_____

1 c. sugar
1/2 c. Flour or 4 T Cornstarch
1/4 tsp salt
Mix together. Separate 3 eggs.
Beat egg yolks into 3 C milk (cold)
Pour into dry ingredients & cook
until thickens.
Add 2 T butter
1 tsp vanilla Stir Pour in baked shell
Add 1/2 c coconut Flour Beat 3 egg
marainge
whites until stiff, add sugar
2-3 T. Sprinkle with cocoaut
Bake until very light brown—

40. Coconut Cream Pie-Delectable

Once you master this pie, you will want to make it all the time. The filling is out of this world, and EVERYONE will want this recipe once your guests taste the creaminess therein.

 Easy

 90-Minutes

Ingredients

1 cup sugar

1/2 cup flour or 4 tablespoons cornstarch

1/4 teaspoon salt

3 eggs (separate the yolk from the whites and use whites for meringue.)

3 cups milk (cold)

2 tablespoons butter

1 teaspoon vanilla

1/2 cup coconut

MERINGUE

3 egg whites

2-3 tablespoons sugar

Preparation

Mix sugar, flour (or cornstarch) and salt. Separate 3 eggs. Beat egg yolks into milk (cold.) Pour into dry ingredients and cook for 2 minutes or until it thickens. Add butter, vanilla, and stir. Add coconut. Pour into a baked pie shell.

MERINGUE

Beat three egg whites until stiff then add sugar. Top pie with meringue. Sprinkle with coconut. Bake at 350 degrees until very light brown.

My Two Cents

This pie was my grandma's specialty baked into a flaky pie crust. You can't beat the taste of this treat. Like any custard filling type dessert, you have to take care to not over or undercook it. Mastering this technique is an art.

NOTES:

_____

_____

_____

Coconut Cream Pie

4 egg slightly beaten
Mix with 1 c sugar
1 c Griffins Waffle Syrup.
(Griffins Prefered)
4 T Butter
1 tsp Vanilla
1½ c pecans
Pour In unbaked Pie crust
bake at 375° 40-45 until Knife clean.

41. Pecan Pie-Sappy

Pecans are prevalent in many parts of the American South which is why we see so many of my recipes with that nut added. There is nothing like the sugary goodness accompanied by the crunch and flavor of this pie. Serve this buttery good Pecan Pie to your guests by using this recipe.

 Easy

 45-Minutes

Ingredients

4 eggs slightly beaten

1 cup sugar

1 cup maple syrup

4 tablespoons butter

1 teaspoon vanilla

1 1/2 cup pecans

Preparation

Mix eggs with sugar and other ingredients. Pour in unbaked pie crust. Bake at 375 degrees for 40-45 minutes until the knife is clean.

My Two Cents

This prize-winning recipe with deep southern roots has graced many a holiday table. The aroma sends one to a happy place, feeling the satisfaction derived from a full belly after eating a third slice of this fabulous pie.

NOTES:

_____

_____

_____

_____

_____

_____

1 unbaked Pie shell
2 eggs, slightly beaten
1 2/3 c. evaporated milk
3/4 c. sugar
1/2 tsp salt
1 tsp cinnamon
1/2 tsp ginger
1/4 tsp cloves, Add 1-15 oz can pumpkin
Mix ingredients in order given. Pour into shell, Bake 15 mins 425°, reduce to 350° for 45 minutes.

42. Pumpkin Pie-Perfect

Pumpkin and cloves, ginger and cinnamon fragrances fill the air as you prepare this during the holiday's or just for dessert. Enjoy a time-honored version of a beautiful fall pie.

 Easy

 60-Minutes

Ingredients

1-15 oz can pumpkin

1 unbaked pie shell

2 eggs, slightly beaten

1 2/3 cup evaporated milk

3/4 cup sugar

1/2 teaspoon salt

1 teaspoon cinnamon

1/2 teaspoon ginger

1/4 teaspoon cloves

Preparation

Mix ingredient to given. Pour into shell. Bake at 425 degrees for 15 minutes then reduce to 350 degrees for 45 minutes.

My Two Cents

My mother made the best pumpkin pie using the combination of these ingredients. Cooked properly it is hard to beat with a dollop of whipped topping.

NOTES:

_____

_____

_____

_____

_____

_____

2 c flour)
1 tsp salt
4 T sugar
3 T oil

1 pkg yeast dissolved in warm water
(1 cup.) Mix into dry ingredients.
Add melted shortening or oil. Knead
lightly til smooth, roll + cut into
biscuits. Place in greased pan
and let rise 1 hour or so. Warm
place. Bake in hot oven 350-400°
until brown.

NOTES:

_____
_____
_____
_____
_____
_____
_____

Yeast Rolls

45. Yeast Biscuit-Grandma Rolls

Everyone that has known my family knows what Grandma Rolls are. They are a unique, flaky roll that differs from a biscuit and a traditional yeast roll. You will find that your family will expect them at every gathering once you introduce them.

 Easy

 120-Minutes

Ingredients

2 cups flour

1 teaspoon salt

4 tablespoons sugar

3 tablespoons oil

1 package yeast

Preparation

Mix yeast in 1 cup of warm water then mix into the dry ingredients. Add melted shortening or oil. Knead lightly till smooth then roll and cut into biscuits. Pour a little oil into the corner of a pan covering each biscuit carefully on each side. Then gently place them next to each other in the pan. Let rise 1 hour or so (see yeast packet for the time) in a warm place (turn the oven to 200 degrees then turn it off once it reaches that temperature) to proof rolls. Bake in hot oven 350-400 degrees until golden brown.

My Two Cents

A secret to the success of this recipe is to make sure your water is at the perfect temperature to activate the yeast (never add salt directly into yeast) as suggested on the package. The second thing that I have learned is NOT to add too much EXTRA flour.

2 tbsp yeast, compressed or dry
1/2 c. lukewarm water
1/2 c. milk
4-5 c. sifted all purpose flour
1/4 c. sugar
2 tsp salt
6 T shortening

Soften yeast in lukewarm water,
scald milk. Cool to lukewarm + add
to yeast. Sift together flour, sugar
+ salt. Cut in shortening, stir
into liquid gradually. Turn out on
floured board. Knead gently. Roll
out to 1/4" thick. Cut + shape
into Parkerhouse rolls. Place on
greased baking sheet. Brush with
melted butter. Cover + let rise in
warm place until double (about 1 hr)
Bake in hot oven (435°) about 15 minutes

46. Yeast Rolls-Quick

Here is another yeast roll for you to enjoy. Your family will love the taste of this traditional Yeast Roll.

Intermediate   120-Minutes

Ingredients

2 packages yeast, compressed or dry

1/2 cup lukewarm water

1/2 cup milk

4-5 cups sifted all-purpose flour

1/4 cup sugar

2 teaspoons salt

6 teaspoons shortening

Preparation

Soften yeast in lukewarm water, scald milk. Cool to lukewarm and add to yeast. Sift together flour, sugar, and salt. Cut in shortening. Stir into liquid gradually. Turn out on floured board. Knead gently. Roll out to 1/4" thick, cut and shape into "Parkerhouse" rolls. Place on greased baking sheet. Brush with melted butter. Cover and let rise in a warm place (heat oven to 200 degrees then turn it off) to proof rolls until doubled in size (about an hour). Bake in a hot oven at 425 degrees about 15 minutes.

My Two Cents

Quick and easy rolls to serve anytime with just about any dish. We love rolls in our family, and this is an alternative to our favorite "Grandma Rolls" passed down for generations. Yeast rolls all have a different flavor and texture.

NOTES:

_____

2 pkg Cherry jello
1 C Dark Sweet cherries
1 C Crushed Pineapple
1 C Pecans
2 Small cokes
  Drain juice of cherries &
pineapple. Add enough water
to mixture of juice to make 2 C
liquid & heat to boiling. Pour over
jello & stir until dissolved. Add
cokes, nuts, cherries & pineapple.
Chill til set.

Jell-O Salads

47. Cola Salad-Zingy

You won't find a taste quite like that of a Jell-O salad with Cola. The combination of fruit makes your mouth water with delight.

 Easy

 30-Minutes

Ingredients

2 package cherry Jell-O

1 cup dark sweet cherries

1 cup crushed pineapple

1 cup pecans

2 small cokes

Preparation

Drain juice off cherries and pineapple. Add enough water to the mixture of juice to make 2 cups liquid and heat to boiling. Pour over Jell-O and stir until dissolved. Add cokes, nuts, cherries, and pineapple. Chill till set.

My Two Cents

The flavor that comes from the cola and sweet cherries is terrific. The texture adds to the appearance when this salad when put into a mold. What a beautiful addition to your table this is.

NOTES:

_____

_____

_____

_____

3 pkg Strawberry Jello
2 C boiling water
1 pkg frozen strawberries
1 C whole cranberry sauce
1 C crushed pineapple
Dissolve jello in boiling water.
Add frozen strawberries, mix well. Add
Cranberry sauce & pineapple with juice

48. Strawberry-Cranberry Jell-O Salad-Beautiful

The colors and flavor of this salad are just amazing. The nuts add to the menagerie of this salad. Your family and friends will be coming back for seconds. It is a beautiful dessert or merely a side for turkey and dressing.

 Easy

 30-Minutes

Ingredients

3 packages strawberry Jell-O

2 cups boiling water

1 package frozen strawberries

1 cup whole cranberry sauce

1 cup crushed pineapple

Preparation

Dissolve Jell-O in boiling water. Add frozen strawberries, mix well. Add cranberry sauce and pineapple with juice.

My Two Cents

Molded Jell-O salads have found a seat at the table alongside any main course. The celebration of flavor will delight your guests.

NOTES:

_____

_____

_____

_____

_____

_____

_____

2 generous cups chopped Chicken
2 firm, tart apples, cut into chunks
3 stalks celery chopped
1/2 c raisins
2 T sugar   and ½ cup nuts
1 T Curry Powder
1 c Sour cream
Juice of 1 lemon
Salt + Pepper to taste

Cook boned chicken breast for 10 minutes in simmering water. Remove + drain.

Meanwhile, chop apples + celery. Place in medium bowl with raisins, nuts + chicken. Mix in sugar, curry powder, sour cream + lemon juice. Blend. Serve on lettuce with hard rolls or Bran muffins.

Curry Dishes
49. Curried Chicken Salad-Tasty

A summer picnic or a party on the patio is the perfect venue for this wholesome salad. The curry adds an extra flare that you and your guests will love.

 Easy

 30-Minutes

Ingredients

2 generous cups chopped chicken

2 firm, tart apples cut into chunks

3 stalks celery (chopped)

1/2 cup raisins

1/2 cups nuts

2 tablespoons sugar

1 tablespoon curry powder

1 cup sour cream

1 lemon (juice)

Salt and pepper to taste

Preparation

Cook, boned, chicken breast for 10 minutes in simmering water. Remove and drain. Meanwhile, chop apples and celery. Place in medium bowl with raisins, nuts, and chicken. Mix in sugar, curry powder, sour cream and lemon juice. Blend. Serve on lettuce with hard roll or bran muffin.

My Two Cents

My mother made this when we lived in Michigan. My McNeil family came from Argyll, Scotland in the early 1800s as Pioneers of Mosa, Middlesex, Ontario, Canada. My dad's father eventually made his way to Pontiac, Michigan in the early 1900s. We spent many years in Michigan living on Lake St. Clair. I recall my mother entertaining by the lake and much praise was given to this light but satisfying, unique Curried Chicken Salad.

NOTES:

Curried Chicken Salad

1 # ground beef, lamb or veal.

5 medium onions

1 # 2 can tomatoes

1 pkg frozen okra or green beans (canned may be used)

1 Bay leaf

3 T Curry Powder (Crosse & Blackwell is best)

1/4 C Shredded Coconut (fresh is preferred (but canned is okay)

Salt to taste (start with 1 tsp)   over

1 tsp cayenne pepper

Method

Brown meat after making small balls & also brown onion. Add curry powder & stir & brown for a moment. Add & tomatoes, okra or green beans, salt, Bay leaf, red pepper & simmer about 30 minutes. Just before serving add coconut. Serve over rice. Side dishes include ① sliced bananas with sugar & coconut ② Chopped cashews ③ Chopped raw vegetables — no dressing. Help to drink cool mouth. Put on plate in order 1. Rice 2. Curry 3. Sour cream 4. bananas & coconut 5. Cashews 6. vegetables. Bread & Butter. Unusual and good!

50. Indian Curry-Ancient

Always a treat to have this dish as it has been in my family longer than I have been alive. After a trip to India in 1959, my aunt and uncle introduced it to us. She made it so well, and I love the combinations and exotic zest that comes from layering the different items.

Intermediate　　120-Minutes

Ingredients

1 pound of ground beef, lamb, veal or chicken

5 medium onions

1 to 2 cans tomatoes

1 package frozen okra or green beans (fresh or canned may be used)

1 bay leaf

3 tablespoons curry powder (Cross and Blackwell is best)

¼ cup shredded coconut (fresh is preferred but canned is okay)

Salt to taste (start with 1 teaspoon)

1 teaspoon cayenne pepper

Preparation

Brown meat after making small balls, also brown onion. Add curry powder and stir and brown for a moment. Add tomatoes, okra or green beans, salt, bay leaf, red pepper (cayenne) and simmer about 30 minutes. Just before serving add coconut. Serve over rice. 1) Side dishes include sliced bananas with sugar and coconut. 2) Chopped cashews 3) Chopped raw vegetables. NO DRESSING. Milk to drink to cool mouth. Put on a plate in order 1) Rice 2) Curry 3) Sour cream 4) Bananas and coconut 5) Cashews 6) Vegetables. Serve with bread and Butter. Unusual and good!

My Two Cents

Indian Curry is a unique recipe that many of my McNeil family members grew to love. My dad's brother and his wife went to India in 1959. It was always a special treat to have my aunt make this for us. Enjoy layering these ingredients and creating your version of this delightful dinner.

About The Author And Editor

Patricia Gilliam, the Editor, is a school teacher and has a culinary gift that is remarkable. She lives in Las Vegas, Nevada with her son Michael Johnson who is a talented professional musician in the same city. Patti and Sheri Savory once were married to "Savory" brothers from Oklahoma. Both of these women have roots in Oklahoma and share experiences in making many of these recipes with their mothers and grandmothers. A force to be reckoned with in the kitchen, Patricia brings her artistic touch to many of the dishes photographed in these pages.

Sheri Savory, the Author, is a Genetic Genealogist, Mother, Grandma, and Baker. She currently lives in Los Angeles, CA with her daughter and two granddaughters. Sheri's ancestors came to America in the early 1600s laying out the streets of Baltimore, MD and many other cities as they pioneered across the country. Along with their pots, pans, dishes, and cookbooks, they brought the traditions of their ancestors. Sheri has traveled from the north to the south from the east to the western reaches of the USA living in 33 of them. Her son Brandon Savory is a talented Chef, Filmmaker, and Sailor that has been out to sea on a 24-foot sailboat since 2016 as he sails around the world. Seachangelog.com. He is an avid supporter of this cookbook working as an advisor regarding the photography Sheri did here. See what these men have cooking as they live off the sea and fish, trap, hunt, can, pickle and preserve all of their food. Sheri's daughter was patient and kind as her kitchen was absconded to make every recipe then photograph them. As a TV Commercial producer Rochelle Savory works long hours and yet finds time to be a dynamic mother full of love and creativity. She has always been a cheerleader regarding her mom's projects and continues to care and encourage her. Sheri's mom taught her to make Tuna Casserole, donuts from scratch, and anything else she inquired about before the age of ten. More importantly, she gave her the opportunity to serve her family the casserole after preparing it alone. Her mom's instruction and love ignited a passion for cooking. Sheri, Demi, Dakota and Patrica hope these recipes bring your friends and family together to create and partake in the foods that were born out of the traditions of the "American South."

Bon appetit!

Index

www.ingramcontent.com/pod-product-compliance
Lightning Source LLC
Chambersburg PA
CBHW040245100426
42811CB00011B/1165